Matt Dunn
Hull

To Rebecca + Jamie, thanks for your support health + happiness to your beautiful family

Matty +

SWITZY

By

Matt Dunn

For Shelley, my wife and hero, Madison and Riley, my reason for living, my family, the foundation for everything I am.

Contents

1. Don't dare go there
2. Seat of my pants
3. Chip bark and climbing frames
4. Two water areas & a metal bar
5. Bike rides with brother and sister in law
6. Pre-season for the ages
7. The original and best Bootcamp
8. A doff of a cap
9. 2 laps of military testing
10. Twins with Mummy
11. Twins with Uncle Mike & Buster
12. Scouting for girls & a lot of tears
13. Snowy on the scene
14. The Mighty Comets
15. Park run chasing the boy
16. The body with a history
17. A Sailor, a Dog, a Ferret & a deck of cards
18. Christmas week nights and then sunshine
19. The Flood

Foreword

As with comedy, family, friendships, relationships and life in general we need a constant. For the educated in comedy this has been the face of Kenny. Who entertainingly had his face painted as a tiger then proceeded to be paraded in shot throughout the rest of the series of Phoenix nights.

For others this a song, a time of year a place to visit in free time or even times when we are down.

For me quite simply my place is Humber Bridge Country Park or, as you are about to learn a place known to us local people as Little Switzerland (Little Switz) – shortened still to just Switzy.

The area began life as a chalk quarry giving the park its hilly and sometimes sheer faces, coupled with on dry summer days an almost white set of footpaths to follows its two trails. In addition to this the mill used to process the chalk still stands to this day and is subject to a restoration order as I make these musings.

However, this is no local area history lesson but a simple series of accounts from a man that was once a boy who has chronologically and mostly literally grown up in these wonderful surroundings.

1

Don't dare go there

The eventually well-trodden path from the family home on Boothferry Estate to Switzy was a mere 2 miles in distance. Detail was, as with many legends given to you by your parents and elder siblings at the time; The as yet unconquered trek would be fraught with dangers that my young mind could not perceive.

You see the younger years of your author were not exactly the type that would fill any parents with confidence in many things; Let alone "playing out" at a disused chalk quarry. Two of said reasons were falling over and splitting my head open in a local park (I maintain heavily medicated to this day; my parents argue to the contrary). Secondly leaving my hand atop a fence on the way back from "7" fields, copying my elder brother and his pals, I did a lot of this. The culmination of these accidents were innumerable hours in the local accident and emergency department, syringe administered anesthetic around and into the cuts. Then stitches applied that to this day I believe were made out of bootlaces. Eight in total made up of three in the head and 5 in the hand wound, for those of you that like me are slave to a detail.

This combination of some pretty well-founded worry from my parents coupled with said urban legend from my elder brother put paid to the then 6-year old's exploration dreams.

I look back on these times in wonderment at what I was allowed to do; Thanking from the bottom of my heart my amazing parents for the attitude that gave my elder brother, younger sister and myself the freedom to learn by experience. An allowance that must have been painful to award in any era.

Now a parent of amazing twins I fight with my inner fears, as I am sure my aforementioned parents did to afford my beautiful pair the same freedom.

I digress, prepare yourself for a lot of this as my mind often flits between a well-oiled machine, to the image of a sleeping donkey once used to depict the brainpower of the great Homer, of Simpson's fame.

Our side of the town and into the fair village of Hessle was going through changes rarely seen globally never mind in our town.

A link road to the M62 from the coast of the A63, to be named after the late, great Clive Sullivan MBE stretched beneath the imposing structure of the Humber Bridge. At its point of opening June 1981 standing proudly as the longest single span on the planet.

The surrounding areas were being transformed as the new road link over the Humber; Albeit tolled, was bringing more than the famed fishing trade to our parts.

My parents Jim and Ann, entrenched in all that is good of our fair town with back stories that would probably fill a book alone and not do justice. In the absence of this I will not attempt that now, only a simple snapshot of the wonderful pair that have never ceased to be there for me.

Jim a tradesman in the engineering sector of the highest regard in the area, coupled with a diverse sporting career and fiercely proud of his fairground heritage. History that when looked back on will show success and standard with very few equals and certainly not many betters.

Ann the matriarch of a whirlwind family, relentlessly supportive of all her family not just her 2 sons and daughter; Mike the eldest, middle man in me and Marissa a stunningly beautiful, iron willed sister to us boys. All of whom to this day fill her heart and diary leaving many in wonder how she fits it all in. But that she does, perpetually. Regularly seen at the finish line, final whistle or decision given to any of the triumvirate of pride and joy she mothers so beautifully.

The walk to this hidden gem was from the estate into the outskirts of the Hessle village, "down drain" until. Prior to the upgrade to the link road a scramble across a British rail Marshalling yard. Latterly a trip across one of several pedestrian or vehicle bridges linking the areas would be an option. The regularity and time span of this passage would see the sad demise of Dunston's shipbuilders. The changing face of a local hostelry from a watering hole for shipbuilders, through a period as a Bier Keller, restaurant and in recent times a gymnasium.

The walk along foreshore itself would see the redevelopment of the historic Hessle RUFC and Cricket club, along with several different ice-cream vendors. Serving as a poignant reminder of how history and future often lay side by side – the now redundant Lincoln Castle, a paddle steamer born from Glasgow and remaining in service until 1978 was moored as a public house on the ever-varying mud banks.

Approaching the breathtaking new span of the estuary into sight came the first of many different versions of tidal defenses, the most modern of which – tempered glass in construction remains in the build phase to this day.

It is at the start of the defence wall that a house unlike any other you are likely to encounter. A building which serves as probably the bedrock of reason for the warning don't dare go there...... .

A house that was to compliment, unkempt and rundown but in straight talking a shithole. A mix of cottage brickwork, rendering, dry rot infested windows rarely of two alike, tired slate roof and an overgrown garden to boot. Worryingly and more eerily was the fact these are the parts of the abode you could see.

The painted word addition to the outside was not on many occasions read in full thanks in simple form to the potential threat of the fabled occupier.

You see when the legend tells that the sole resident is a "Manwoman" pairs with story of a murder being committed in said building is more than enough for the cessation of any plan to visit a flooded chalk pit.

Now in times where diversity was certainly not a dance troupe, nowhere near a movement of rainbow colouring. More probable it was demonstrated by a male returning from the bar with a drink for the missus that had a cherry in it. The acceptance of what in all probability was a transvestite was a distant second to the alleged murder.

Either or, this dual legend was enough to strike a fear into me that would last long into my teenage years. A fear that still presents a little anxiety to this day as I stare into the empty void where the long since demolished house stood.

In fairness to both my memory and the legends that formed much of that. When I look at the evidenced prime location that lay undeveloped there must have been a level of truth in the dark past of this place.

2

Seat of my pants

What seemed like an age passed and the joyous union of being deemed old enough and slowly securing a place as in my brother's gang. A unison that meant it was time to pop my larking out cherry. Per chance to leave the relative safety of our tenfoot (a concrete roadway at the rear of a row of houses used primarily as access for the local binmen. To access garages of the abodes and always a place of relative safety for the kids of the area – so named as it was 10 feet wide), shake off the shackles of the until now leap of faith that was a trip to Gower Park and make comparative trek to Switzy.

Nerves mixed with uncertainty; questions raced in my young mind. Would Manwoman be seen? What would we do, would I make a hat trick of injuries, and how were we getting there? How long could we be gone before getting "chowed at"? remained dominant in my young mind.

Such was my tender years that having a bike of any description was fantasy, the permission to ride it so out of bounds an impossibility. When the older boys of the gang showed up on Grifters and BMX's the trip had already becoming more daunting before leaving our tenfoot.

At two and a half years older than me although my big brother and pretty much inspiration he was not in any way untouchable. The man I looked to as my eyes into a future I had no idea what would hold, stood by no means eldest in his peer group, yet to me was all I needed for a lead.

The chat the elders were having, banter if you will be way over and above anything, I had been involved prior and to a large degree would encounter for many years and experiences to come. Nerves built ever stronger as the trip continued.

Leaving the relative crutch of our tenny moving toward the first of the drain cut throughs. It was becoming obvious that our route would take in the old marshalling yard and a dash across the prepared aggregates of the soon completed A63.

A route that caused worry owing to the ever unpredictability of the Hessle water table. Which in short could withstand a week's rain with no less than a puddle on a road. Yet a short downpour would leave many of the fields surrounding the village nothing short of a bog.

First hurdle was the layout of the marshaling yard then onto Livingstone road itself, once negotiation of the field was relatively successfully completed. Just a trainer full of muddy water and a bit of muck on my hands – our pace quickened as the tarmac run into the country park area stretched out in front of us.

This run along with its obvious landmarks is one of genuine beauty, huge trees lining all of its several routes along. Almost completely hidden behind an impressive copse was the track of the Hessle Cycle Speedway Club. Brilliant white pavilion, orange red cinder track, banked at the corners, start tapes fluttering in the estuary side wind and a number of boys and girls going through warm ups and shiny fixed wheel cycles of all colours imaginable.

Subject matter at this point of the conversation switched as it does in all junior times that being one of the lads claiming he was county standard but didn't want to carry on. Yet in uncharacteristic honesty a contradictory cry you wouldn't get me anywhere near a bike with no brakes. A phrase that triggered a rare moment of unity as we exclaimed (with varying expletives – we were estate lads after all) NO Brakes!!!!!!!!!

This interlude now brushed off we returned to our mission of getting to Switzy, again testing my already well charted nervous disposition the new chat was in regard to the legend of Manwoman. Only this time the elders – as they will become known – were planning to get a "chase on" from the fabled occupant of that house.

Now not that I am not looking for a challenge, that is what being a kid is all about but best part of 3 years younger than the rest of a group. As I stood with one foot with the extra weight of a fish supper. Three of the other four out on bikes my attention switched to being caught by a then believed mythical creature, that fekkin murders people.

Luckily for me the occupier clearly didn't fancy chasing a group of loudmouth young kids and stayed in whilst we chuntered on by.

A quick look through five pockets full of shrapnel confirmed that we had nowhere enough money for a Penna's ice cream and onward to our destination it was.

Loosely fenced off railway line, yet more stunning trees and what seemed pile after pile of chalk-based rubble met us as we left the North tower behind us.

This area that was to become my go to place for so many different reasons struck in no way a reference to how it looks now.

As we approached the inner ring of the park and the lads who sat aside their bikes got off, we perched unsteadily on a sheer face of loose at best, quarried chalk. Many trees littered the drop but having already being made aware of my luck many times at my tender years I was pretty certain that I wouldn't hit any of em. More than likely ending up in the drink at the bottom, leaving my fate to my non-existent swimming skills.

Even with all the impetuousness of youth of our group on our collective side this was not a viable entry point to the undiscovered layout below. As we navigated our way round the top ring in search of a better opening, a bonus would be found that all youth will appreciate. A previous "gang" if you will, had found combination of materials – a rope and a branch to form a swing.

This simplistic piece of outdoor engineering requires no stress testing, no load bearing stamp and certainly no safety certificate as it is and forever will be tested by the youngest in the group. Up I stepped to my first chance to prove myself in this budding clan. My still dirty hands struggled with the roughness of the branch causing grazing to my palms which I had no intention of letting on about. I clambered uncomfortably atop the branch and just about to some sort of balance when the expected over zealous pushing began. As the fear of falling off said swing paled into insignificance alongside the gilt-edged opportunity of being accepted. Whilst being a long way from encouraging the ever-increasing thrusts – only matched by the howls of delight from below I accepted up to the point of inevitable disaster.

Hard as I tried to cling one particularly aggressive shove saw my questionable balance finally defy me and me plummet to the loose chalk below. Thankfully I landed on my backside which aside from pushing me ever closer to a reprimand from my parents caused no real damage. Several rotations of howling older kids each trying to go higher, faster and of course for longer on the swing followed. Leaving this we looked for a different angle of attack to the joys of below.

This line of attack was made bizarrely at a point nowhere near any trees and with a straight run downhill into the water of unknown depth or content below.

The well-versed difference of years in the group produced some very different descents – surfing, running even rolling were witnessed what seemed to be flying past me on the way to a small but sufficient flat area before the water. I had no such skills or style and planned to descend on both feet in full squat in the forlorn hope of being able to stand up at the clearing. Many reasons raced through my head why this was one hell of a lot of stupid ideas I had mustered. These thoughts soon disappeared as I rocked back on to the seat of my pants, dirty and grazed young hands no help on a loose chalk cliff. Heading through the clearing with clear certainty there was no possibility of any help stopping me hurtling toward a splash landing. Chest thumping, mind racing, cheers of delight from my "mates", wet feet and all served as distraction to the fact that I had finally worn through the seat of my pants which in all honesty had lasted a lot longer than I ever expected.

Now the fear of returning like Stig of the dump from a day larking out was a regular occurrence even in our small zones of activity, but returning with no arse in your strides was a different matter completely.

Manwoman was now an option worth taking for lodging compared to the wrath of your parents faced with another shopping trip to stop their son looking like a tramp! For whatever god looked upon us the return journey was swift, the reception was fairly tame and the bath was surprisingly lacking in its usual fire given the lack of skin following the day's activities.

In all my Switzy virginity had now gone and a love affair started that would never leave me……….

3

Chip bark and climbing frames

Enjoying my development and sitting solidly into double figures I found confidence growing with each venture away from the traditional areas of play. Long was the time since I had shaken the shackles of my brothers' elder group and begun my time in my own peer group.

A small but tight knit set of mates, some from the estate others from further afield and the glorious, underappreciated streets of Gyspyville.

The route into Switzy was now unrecognisable to what I had encountered in my early visits. Adding to the dominant landmarks of the rugby club, tidal barrier and of course the bridge; (at this time about to slip from top spot in single span with the Akashi Kaikyo Bridge in Kobe, Japan nearing completion), houses and B&Bs

were sprouting up. Also underway was a new base for the Humber Rescue team literally in the shadow of the North Tower.

Feeling that I had some form of tour guide role I would often lead the walk into the area telling of the history that I knew and unsurprisingly glossing over anything I had little idea about.

No matter how often we used the foreshore front as our entry, many others by this point were available I would spend extra time and emphasis on the legend of Manwoman.

Sadly, the house regardless of how much of the tales you believed stood in a dilapidated state. The only nod to the stories of past being a large board of political ramblings regarding squatting and owners' rights to the outer of the building. Even that almost covered by the overgrown bushes that fronted the house.

Entry to the now well-developed park was via two tunnels that were both lacking in light; the second of which made you more than a touch claustrophobic and should the timing clash with a passing train overhead a feeling like you were under attack.

The loose chalk sheer walls were almost now eradicated, clad now in several trees, shrubs and soils left from several minor shifts in the rock. Pathways of white crushed chalk and limestone branched off in many directions.

Gone were the days of this only being a playground for the brave and foolhardy for the once little discovered gem had been as good as pedestrianised.

Hand carved solid wood markers sat in the stone at every junction of pathway, families snaked through our playground with bamboo handled fishing nets, coupled with buckets or jam jars in the hope of a successful session of newting in one of two water areas.

It was however an early link up between the Humber Bridge Board and the local East Riding of Yorkshire council that was drawing the numbers in at this time.

You see in the points of the year that the mass of trees in Switzy were covered in leaves, this makes for a canopy like very few other. The estuary regularly brings to the foreshore a wind that was consistently brutal in its power. However due to the sheer faces formed by the mining history of this area and the tress' leafy cover Switzy pretty much has its own microclimate.

These conditions made for a great site for one of the only adventure playgrounds in the area for the local youth to entertain itself upon. More tree bark chippings than you could imagine was the bed for a wooden jungle gym. This was a foundation for netting of the brightest orange ropes formed into nets and tunnels providing tests that never seemed to be the same.

Kids of all ages traversed the frames and tunnels slipping between the relative solidity of a tunnel which was decked by footplates made of solid wood. These rat runs were suspended from equally robust yet heavier gauge wood to looser rope sections that left your feet feeling as if they were falling through.

A staple guarantee of any session on the frame was that you were going to be trodden on by a fellow adventurer. Leaving your only hope it was a meatier part of your body that took the pressure rather than the discomfort of a hand or foot.

Either way the shrill of laughter was heard throughout the park or I swear to this day nobody ever really knew where the activity was located, they just followed the noise until a clearing appeared and its bright structure came into sight.

As curiosity met bravery the standard ascent of this at height maze disappeared to be replaced by a more spontaneous and unplanned clamber that more often than not ended in the much more rapid descent onto the bark below.

Looking back, it was never really confirmed to any of regular users of this shining light of a playground why the climbing frame vanished as quickly as it arrived but that it most certainly did.

With the benefit of hindsight and experience I dare say if I was betting a pound from my pocket. A combination of numerous injuries on an unsupervised area, coupled with the lack of maintenance for the frame would be my flutter.

The swift removal had no effect to wipe any memories of this short-lived activity. Only a few weeks prior to beginning of writing this offering. I was asked by a lady of similar age to myself as to whether I recalled the area and we shared with fondness how busy the area was in this short but great time.

Similar to so many other places of natural fun generating sites to the memory bank it was sent to be recalled only by those lucky to have been around at the time.......

4

Two water areas & a metal bar

The years had advanced; the indecisiveness of tender years had been replaced with an adolescent confidence. I was at this time every inch young man in waiting. Hairstyles had been experimented with – blonde streaks arguably the worst, however a flat top attempt on a covering that was one percent away from an afro also had a rating in the archive of do's. I stood at an athletic five feet 10 inches at this point, owing much to the genetics from my family, but also from an at the time dual sports career. These were namely Karate and Rugby League, two areas in which I hold huge regard but was about to split due to my first call up into representative rugby.

This split would see the end of my Karate career and the development of my embryonic Rugby League exploits.

The latest foray into Switzy was a lot more planned than previous jaunts, this was for many reasons. A recent recce confirmed that both water areas were prime for a dip, the exact period in our lives was during those heady long, hot, school time summer holidays.

The planning included money for ice cream, a towel to dry off from the expected wet and a better pair of kegs (best does not exist when you are 12-year-old....), in addition to this was a more than regular application of body spray. The reason for this over planning was that this particular visit was in the company of girls.

Now having a face that turned more stomachs than heads, at this point in my youth any attention was more than welcome.

I was pretty certain that said attention was from the side of me being a good mate, a compliment in itself. Any chance was not going to be under appreciated by a youngster whose hormones were racing at a level only a juiced-up Ben Johnson at that year's Olympics could match.

The walk passed in a heartbeat in the mid-summer heat, no history lesson on this occasion and certainly no reference to the run-down abode of a legendary transvestite.

Brilliant white chalk paths cut through lush green patches of wild grass that were yet to be scorched by the summer sun. We weaved in and out of shade provided by the canopy of leaves as the trees of Switzy stood proudly at their most burdened with greenery. As quick as we had met, we were now in the bowl of the park.

Surrounded by the rough white façade of the bowl we stood and looked out at two water areas, ripples from a light breeze across the surface of water that on a day as beautiful was as inviting as it was clear.

Me and a mate flanked by 2 of the better proportioned girls in our year, clothed loosely at best, looking back maybe even suggestively. The whirlwind of thoughts that I am sure consumed my mates mind as they were mine was leading to a similar question – will we be joined in the water by these two, and of course would we get a look at a bit more……….

The wait was short for answers as following a few playful tossing of loose items into the drink said stones and sticks were soon joined by all four of us for a brief yet owing to my base level of experience in any of this type of event a simply unforgettable moment.

It was following the exit of the girls from the water that I was to gain one of many scars to adorn my fluctuating sized body. I stayed with my mate in said drink – for those of you that know the park it was the smaller of the two water areas we were left in. Probably as my awareness of the depth of the larger water area and potential to make a tit out of myself was far greater and I had steered us this way.

What was about to be proven was that the earlier throwing of stones etc. into the water was to be but a starter to the main course. A projectile that I was about to be hit with, not that I would see it coming only to feel it.

Stood wide legged up to the knees in clear but cold water, sun beating down on my back staring out planning my next vain attempt at impressing our company for the day. I became aware of several wails and screams from behind my back which I put down to the entirely plausible possibility of my mate finding it easier to speak to the girls better than my pathetic attempts at peacocking.

My head full of thoughts of the next headlong dive probably stopped my full awareness but the sudden impact of a solid metal bar between the shoulder blades had all the necessary mind sharpening I required. An act coupled with had the added bonus of attention I could not have dreamed of.

Now dreamed is of course a strange terminology when you are pissing wet through; nightmare would be closer as not even half dressed and at the behest of three schoolmates who are tending to a what could be huge cut or graze as their "care" was giving sweet FA away to be frank.

When experiencing previous issues, to return home and faced confessing to your parents the events of the day. The prospect of producing a cut down the middle of your back isn't a favourable one.

Now fortunately some questionable first aid skills on scene with the aid of a nearly sterile towel – it had only dried the pond water off prior to being used as makeshift gauze. In addition, a wash at one of the now plentiful number of toilet facilities at the park, not always clean but sufficient, I was as fixed as I was going to get on the way home.

The trip home was certainly a lot more concerned than the carefree summers jaunt that got us there a couple of hours earlier.

You see being from a family of playing it safe and now being literally painfully aware of the injury and probable infection that a cut and exposure to stagnant water had almost certainly left me with. The prospect loomed of dreaded of all suggestions / instruction was surely awaiting me on my return of – "he will need a tetanus".

Now an impressive number of early year's injuries that yielded said injection as cover for these infections also gave me an intrinsic knowledge of how long the tetanus lasted for. At this time local advice was five years and the notion of top ups following injuries had not been muted, so of all my ensuing panics to face this was not one of them. Whether I was to be listened to with my logic remained to be seen.

My entry in the Dunn home was met with an understandably irate father and concerned mother who although was more than well versed in the art of profanities. I had already witnessed several DIY attempts that pushed him to turning the air blue; a particular story of rewiring a light fitting which would fill a chapter had this book, being about the home of our family. When in times of concern or particular ire my Dad would slip into a mantra of complete avoidance of swear words. An eerie calm if you will and a presentation that would leave you in no uncertainty that what he was about to say was to be followed to the letter.

So, on the surface to a stranger the phrase "it's always best to get these sorts of things checked out" I knew full well was a clear directive that a trip to Hull Royal Infirmary accident and emergency awaited. As did the inevitable four hours wait and needle your gran could knit with, hopefully going into my arm not, as legend would have me believe, up my backside.

In what had started out as the chance for a sundrenched day of activity never had in such company before. Ended staring around a tired casualty ward with the only entertainment the local drunk or late arrival from a fight at last orders of the areas drinking hole. Providing pretty much a blueprint of future exploits in my luckless early times.

5

Bike rides with brother and sister in law

Times with my amazing brother Mike, hold a dominant place in the chapters of this book and for that no apologies are made. Only hope that I can do his memory justice he so richly deserves. His life was varied, wonderful and packed with activity that left many in awe of not just his achievements but his ability to fit in his schedules.

A close family friend in eulogy of my brother quoted the following "it is not the amount of years in your life, but the amount of life in your years – to which you should be most proud". Rarely before or since in the life of this great has a quote rang so true.

As years progressed my brother and I grew more than aware, that our time as a partnership in our bedroom was quickly coming to an end.

Aside from a number of physical bust ups that would probably register on the Richter scale we had literally shared our life from that room. Rarely was a split in size despite the difference in years and as such clothes were pooled more than divided. Not that Mike ever agreed to this it was just the way it happened!

The activity split had also shown our differences as Mike pushed onwards in his Karate career, already at this point a national champion. I following my Rugby League career, also yielding a few representative honours myself but of course nothing at the level my brother was achieving.

This in mind as Mike declared his first serious relationship, I was full of worry that would be the divisive wedge that we would struggle to recover from.

To expand on the declaration, I was not fully descriptive of my understanding of his blossoming partnership. The story details as awaiting my turn to read the evenings Hull Daily Mail (Dad first then age order following), Mike gave away his feelings for his future wife with a very simple statement that appeared at the time lost on my Mum and Dad.

His current place of employment – Kingston Training Workshops had a write up in paper following a visit earlier in the month. His statement? Went as such "typical they have spelled her name wrong here". Upon closer inspection a photo of a person clad in gauntlets and welding mask in the workshop was titled; Ike Tichopad demonstrates her skills in the welding workshop.

Why's that I enquired knowingly? It's HEIKE, my brother's curt response. As all good brothers are implored to do, I stored it as ammo for a later point.

Thing is the combined worry of the imminent split in our brotherly co-habitation and my eagerness to use the aforementioned grammar police moment, kind of cancelled each other out. What actually happened following the excruciating announcement to our parents Mike moved to involve me in everything he possibly could when away from Heike. A move which served to assist in my development into the fittest I had ever been going into my final year in junior as all of our involvements were training based.

The rub of this refreshed partnership was the day that my brother asked me if I wanted to go for a bike ride. Five or so years prior this request would have been straightforward notion and acceptance. The facts of the length of time it had been since a similar activity, the company – with his new partner. The location? Where else but the playground of Switzy sent me into a delightful frenzy and became the ultimate offer I could not refuse.

So, the date set, a new bike more than ready for a test run, the day a stunning Summer morning and a scene set for what would be known in more modern times as a bonding day. In honesty this was not required as anyone that was good enough for my brother was good enough for me.

Now strangely on a day that was presenting with such promise, all of my previous nerves and worries were racing back. This was due in no small part to the fact that in my embryonic knowledge of this couple's activities being of a thrill-seeking nature. Plus having never actually cycled around the park myself, the strong possibility was that I faced another day of making a tit out of myself.

What in fact played out was a day that rightfully takes its place alongside the other recollections was a stunning day that would again put the modern snowflake society in meltdown.

The three of us spent in the absence of chat but in a bond of activity and exhilaration lasting hours turning these well-trodden paths. With many off-track areas made into a run that to this day I don't believe had been cycled before. Hard work, definitely, fun undoubtedly and more for the log of unforgettable times in this corner of joy, a certainty.

6

Pre-season for the ages

The scene of the next recall from Switzy was in fairness over 13 years in the making and in all honesty the first time that over-confidence would betray me as opposed to the trepidation that had consumed me on the majority of my previous visits.

All my formative years were now a thing of the past, my memorable years as a 'Boys Club lad had passed. A couple of attempts at making the grade at the two professional clubs our town boasts, firstly Hull FC and latterly Hull KR had ended ultimately without success. A lot of fun was had but the honesty that would serve me so well in the rest of my life helped me accept my career lay outside the paid ranks.

To a famous night in the local – Norland – sat with the great that is Pete Jordan watching live Rugby League in the form of Wigan v Leeds and having my beer bought all night. Setting the scene for a love affair that would last in playing the next 13 years, in reality would never leave me. These years would see me graduate from the "A" team, a period in which I was described eloquently as "second to bonny" – not a compliment believe me in our Kings town, into a regular that played alongside some of the very best ever in the amateur game.

It was after 2 years at the club and approaching my third pre-season that I was approached by the committee to ask of my brothers' availability to "do a bit of fitness work". After an invitation like this a few things go through your mind, firstly the chance for you to have your brother show his skillset was never going to be a problem. Secondly this is a major chance to announce yourself to the club on and off the playing field and of course lastly if I had a quid in my pocket, I would bet two that the venue for our "bit of fitness" was going to be Switzy.

Now one of the greatest things of being an amateur in Hull is that when you hit the beer you link up with pretty much a complete cross section of the other clubs and get the news from their particular camps. Plus, if this was a bit sparse one weekend the Monday morning return to the caravan manufacturers, factories or indeed office tea rooms sure got you up to speed.

High on the list of the chat was that some crazy bloke in tight fitting Lycra had rocked up at West Hull (one of, if not the finest amateur sides in the town). To run a Tuesday session that left the players in such a state with his shenanigans that the Thursday session was cancelled. That Lycra clad nutter was of course none other than my brother.

Now the fair club of Norland was historically one of the best attended sides for pre-season but then come Hull Fair and the clocks changing, inevitably coupled with the worsening weather saw our numbers drop off. Armed with this knowledge and more than the usual weekly banter around the workplaces the concern was that the session at Wests would scare our lads off.

But that balmy Tuesday night yielded a turn out that I don't think was ever surpassed in the following 10 years give or take. Top car park was awash with tanned frames, in clothing of colours akin to a psychedelic dream, classic nineties hair style and an age range spanning close on 20 years. Confidently striding amongst the players was yours truly, now feeling fully at home in his club and doing his best to present as the player that was to breeze this session.

Unbeknown to us our Mike was already here plotting, scheming even, to give us around Switzy as much – if not more than he gave Wests a couple of weeks ago. As us players were turning nerves into banter his image appeared from the stair's entry to Switzy and as he bellowed for us to join him the nerves returned in abundance. There are many intricacies to my late great brothers' character but of the most dominant are the following; he loved an audience; he was an incredible judge of how his session is going.

Playing to said crowd was so natural I sometimes wonder if he missed a calling in life but his ability to spark them was unparalleled across the fitness world. You see not only did Mike do exactly what everyone else was doing (a common approach amongst the leading lights in the industry) he had the ability and fitness to traverse a full group. Moving from the lead participants, through the middles in the grey areas whilst never forgetting those at the back, often getting better results than even the most optimistic thought possible.

It was once said that it was all in the smile, whilst agreeing I took a slightly different angle on this. My slant being it was the how he communicated with the smile. You can say all the right things to your group, captive audience or not but if you say it through gritted teeth, misplace your expletive, shout when you needed to speak powerfully all the effort is lost. That criticism was never levelled to Mike.

The next hour and a half – that felt like an eternity – served to unite a group of players by testing their resolve, forcing them to work together in partners and groups they had rarely worked in, making them hurt whilst making them laugh through it all, leaving an impression that would last throughout the careers and in some cases lives of the group who attended the session.

The level of achievement from both the playing group as we scaled fences, scrambled the much-lauded chalk faces of the park, ascended innumerable numbers of steps, carried one another uphill and down dale. All the while completing a glut of bodyweight exercises would not be possible without a certain level of bastard – even with it I can assure you many felt like giving up.

Well if that attitude was needed in the players it is simply the lifeblood of being the man my brother was. Like most of us when showing that steel a little of our dark side would glint through those eyes and believe I was more than aware of how it would manifest that night.

When fatigued – we were definitely that – two major areas dissipate very quickly your ability to communicate (we'll come back to that later in the book) and more obviously your form in whatever you are performing. So, as I skipped a couple of reps of the latest bodyweight move ordered by the man himself. I felt a presence alongside me and instantly I fell into the feeling that hurt me the more than so many others. Shame overcame me that my own brother was disappointed in me, was I the worst in form – nowhere near, was I the only player skipping reps – not a chance. But that was not what was been looked for in this session as Mike was looking to instill virtues in my training that would last a lifetime and I can confirm that simple presence did that. To this day I find myself performing extras in any session I do. Flawed in the belief that eight years after his passing I can avoid any disappointment in me by him.

The shower back at home was one of the finest I had ever enjoyed, the next one not even close to enjoyable and to be honest for a couple of days it hurt to breathe.

Foundations for a stellar season set and an approach to training galvanised in this pre-season for the ages.

7

The original and best Bootcamp

At the time of this book being conceived even in our small town at the end of a road. You will find well into double figures fitness instructors offering their version of the fantastic offering that is a Bootcamp. They will have you indoors, outdoors, on field, in sports halls. Furnished with kettle bells, coloured bibs, group leaders et al. Every single one of these sessions are doing something that so many previous fads and fashions that preceded them failed to do – they are keeping people engaged in regular activity and all kudos to them for doing that.

Similar to the first telephone, TV set and motor vehicle all other versions are duty bound to be compared to the first.

In a dreamlike partnership of the country park and my brother, this time with a very close circle of friends and family form the gym and work the areas original and of course best Bootcamp was born.

Simple rules exist,

- Don't be late
- Nobody pays
- Every single person of any ability is welcome, including your dogs
- If you miss 3 sessions you are out
- You work to the best of your ability

Like all great systems and processes the starts are humble – think Nissen hut dwelling scientists finding cures and inventions. Plus, in another nod to those greats of our creative past it may not have been 99% perspiration and 1% inspiration but it surely sees some sweat.

The blood and tears took more than a small part too but always in the greatest spirit of what makes any session a worthwhile one. Willing participants, taking a genuine interest in each other's well-being, a multitude of abilities all catered for and encouraged to attend, even our canine co-runners.

The meeting was/is 0715hrs for 0730hrs start Saturday mornings, born out of the one of the greatest quotes I have ever worked to "5 minutes early is 10 minutes late". Have the audacity to turn up late and an already testing warm up would become close on unbearable. To my knowledge there was literally no exceptions to when his group would train, any weather, any date the session could be adjusted to suit.

Laps of one of the car parks at our disposal would soon explode into life as the ring master would bellow out a change of pace, pause the lap to begin an exercise or simply to increase the pace. We would then take off on dry days into the park itself to uncover a loot hidden at the end of the previous week's session that would include weights belts fashioned into harnesses to pull tyres, 5 gallon water cans, weight bars and anything else that would give an extra level of resistance whilst navigating a seemingly never ending number of ways through the park.

Now of course alongside the most obvious of resistance which was your own fatigue levels. Mad Mike (one of many of the more polite names he would be called throughout these sessions) would naturally employ the age-old hamper of another person to test the resolve of his willing subjects.

A more than regular sight for the early Saturday dog walkers would be his group scaling hills and steps linked in piggy back or even fireman's carry. Don't let the agricultural nature of this session fool you into a notion that this was not scientific. This hour was as structured as any test or period being thrown across professional sports clubs and University departments the country over.

An intrinsic knowledge of not just the number of steps but how many were in each section of an ascent or descent. Serve well as substance to his everlasting encouragement and also fill the banter between his more combative participants. The ever-smooth transition between steps, to carries, to incline running although maintaining your work in a lactic threshold. Whilst also keeping your tanks full enough to not fall apart or even injure. Did accidents happen? hell yes, at the end of the day this was a group of up to twenty people running effectively off road in conditions that could genuinely see all four seasons in one go.

In addition to the challenge of his plans for the aforementioned combatants was the option to divert his less able team members to stay involved but take a shorter route. Rejoining knowing they had been tested to their own limits. In itself a talent to give the comfort that is not only a testosterone fueled challenge. This was art form by a man consumed, living his life in the most active, engaging and empowering way he could.

A personal favourite of yours truly was the hill running sector, done in the main on a tarmac incline at the end of a flat green area. A life in Rugby League started at the Hull Boys Club, whose go to training session was on dock side sand hills gave me a particular ability in running uphill. This was in no means a chance for me to show my pace – I was comfortably in the grey on this – but it was in endurance that I came into my own. Setting off toward the owls that denoted the two-thirds way up markers saw even the most athletic tighten up. With a mix of form and pig headedness I would maintain my pace and pass many of the group that if we were on the flat, I would be happy to still see them within a similar distance.

My attendance of this session was more fleeting then constant and back to fleeting dependent on whether I was in season at Norland or working. This is where I probably used nepotism in its purist form to ensure I was not exited on the missing attendance rule. Now along with the group knowing what my relationship was to their receptive leader. I know that I left nothing in the tank on any of these hours, often picking up extras to ensure my acceptance. Of course, I needn't have concerned myself in this as tight knit community welcomed me each time with an outpouring of emotion that would have the recent social distancing brigade having kittens.

When you have lived all of your brother's countless achievements to see what he meant to these people probably summed him and what we did in our playground up the in the purist way. In fairness to the others that have spawned from this most original of Bootcamps I observe a real community that builds. Maybe from arrogance, maybe pure love I don't see these groups celebrate and mourn in the way this one continues to do to this day. This is catalogued in a post session breakfast at a local pub or café, obligatory cards of celebration or commiseration. The most staple of all birthday treats, whoever's birthday it was and of course number – no ladies did not get away with twenty-one - called the exercise and that's how many the team finished the workout with.

8

A doff of cap

One of many returns to the church that was Switzy was in recovery from one of several injuries that would not blight my chosen career in Rugby League but would certainly leave my pre-seasons a lottery as to whether I hit the ground running.

However forever in my armoury was the ever-available sweat fest of the previously explained Bootcamp. With it an opportunity to lift physical fitness and ability to withstand adversity like no other.

As most things do the sessions had moved on – new kit to play with, higher levels of strength and fitness evident from the group, new members of the group to impress all serving as great bonuses for a man desperate to get the greatest benefit from his latest return.

Now a long-standing golden rule in the world of amateur Rugby League was that Saturdays were in essence holy ground. If there was a game you were expected to move heaven and earth to be available for the game and after match shenanigans of course. More importantly if you were out of season nothing happened on a Saturday.

This considered I was in as good of shape as I could be as I was well rested from my Tuesday, Thursday pre-season on Syd Smith school running track and ready to hit this hour as hard as I possibly could.

From the start much had changed, still measured, still progressive but now we were straight into the park for a short sharp hit to get the pulses racing and almost straight away hitting a threshold in our individual abilities. Maybe it was an early nod to my questionable levels of fitness that steeled me for an assault on the session or just my character. Either way a wake-up call of the highest was given inside five minutes or commencing. A lad who I had the pleasure of coaching at junior level broke his own question of do I get much running in now by answering himself with "clearly not".

A metaphorical red rag had been waved and an opportunity to prove myself was now been sought like a proverbial heat seeking missile.

This would take some time to manifest as said new toys would take up a good half hour with power bag carries, drops, water can carry in unison with loop running was keeping me away from my strong suits.

One thing I had in my locker for the remaining twenty-five minutes of the session was that new kit and extra running aside and appreciated at some point we would return to the more old school hill runs and steps.

The presentation of the content can change as often as it likes – I like many others don't like change. One thing that never changes is the number of steps around the place and the length / gradient of the tarmac hill. If you are wondering entry steps off top car park through the kissing gate are 99, from lower car park turning right before the sweep for the Bridge entry it is 16 very long concrete steps that cause more than a couple of changes in stride pattern. At the base of the 99 there are 31 leading to the two water areas which really do vary in tread length and depth completed with at the other end of the water area are two sets of steps that number at 33 each – all of which were due to be hit in this remainder of session.

Forgive me a digression here if you would – I did warn of this earlier on – but what was about to happen at the end of the 99 steps has roots far away from the chalk bowl of Switzy.

You see many of the Bootcamp team; dogs and all, would also meet up in the Triton Inn car park of a weekend morning and set about a true hill session that was at times close to fell running. This particular session would see the pain of Spout Hill ascended within the first half mile of what could be anything up to an eight, nine or even ten miler. With the potential to hit six hills of genuine challenge within the run dependent on the distance. It was only much later in life; from my now regular running wife did I find out that the renowned City of Hull athletic club consider the six hills as one of their toughest training runs.

The build up to the rub of this story was as structured as all other elements in this catalogue of progression. Starting at four miles, moving through six, then onto the eight, nine and eventual double figures. As most regular trainers will testify to once the mythical double figures are broken the majority of subsequent runs are completed with a steel and point of reference. A steel that not only informs you have how far you are going but how you completed the prior runs.

The day arrived for our longest run but not without a couple of characteristic challenges and motivations from the man himself. Up spout hill, across to the church, on the road the obligatory wave of appreciation between the group and the oncoming cars as we mutually gave way to one another. Over next hill round the house – keeping the country code of course; should there not be a stile gate to clamber over the gate would be chivalrously opened and closed as the group passed – through a copse not without a challenge underfoot. Next passing the farmhouse with the resident Collie giving her usual encouragement. Along the airfield, into further woodland this time with a downhill, a dash across a road and onto Mount Airy into more cover of a wooded canopy, along the top walkway alongside the quarry. This was usually coupled with a rasp of a crosser or two using the natural moguls left by the diggers and onto a track toward Weadley Springs. It was at this point the muscle memory was disappearing and my previous best of 10 miles was about to obliterated as we clearly weren't using the water area as our previous turnaround.

Instead onto areas I had not seen previously, nor since to be fair and then snaking back to more familiar surroundings.

The brother had been, as always doing his front to back and vice versa laps and at the point of his latest pause. He looked up with a glint in his eye and quipped "turn right and home or turn left down to that 30mph sign (it was just about visible) and make a u turn then it's a half marathon".

HALF MARATHON?!? Shock left an instant and my legs almost uncontrollably turned left overtaken by a sense of need to complete soon to be hitting the distant marker that carried me to our origin of Triton Car Park. Many were already completing post run stretches as I laboured home to see the figure of Mike glance down at his Garmin, report "two hours four minutes our kid". Then with that, make a gesture that meant more than anything – he doffed an imaginary cap at my achievement. In the years since and additional weight plus inevitable injuries I have not bettered that time on or off road, but this appreciation of my effort was my greatest medal.

Returning to Switzy and my latest of a sporadic attendance of the Bootcamp and my efforts to catch the questioner of my dwindling running ability we were by all estimations approaching the last leg of the workout. We had finished with the resistant work just a run back with the kit left now, the concrete steps had been hit a fair number of times meaning that our most likely of exit points would be what is to become Uncle Mikes steps – 99 steps of lung busting ascent. These are split into five mini sectors each tempting you to look up to see how far you have left to go, a move that is met with peril as you never seem to be getting closer as fatigue overpowers effort.

At the base of the steps we paused a moment to divvy up the items that had been carried, dragged and pushed for the last hour prior to our final effort.

As the original carrier of the two five-gallon water cans I was, in a show of fairness offered a spell on the ascent by one of the team. Whom were tasked with a smaller item. Now think back to my confession of pig headedness matching if not beating ability and you can probably predict my items to carry were the most awkward, heavy and challenging. So, my response to the offered assistance was deliberate decline with a look that Mrs. Dunn describes as "wanting to kill someone".

For all your fans of motivational films and the Rocky films in particular I would have loved this to be a Rocky III moment; as I chase the superior athlete down our metaphorical beach and catch him in the last throws of our session. But you see of all my characteristics, dominant throughout is a sense of brutal honesty, I was never going to catch him irrespective of the kit he or I was carrying. My aim now was to complete the session as strongly as I possibly could. This was a lesson that many years later would be put into words by a young professional Rugby League player in the town who shared this quote "I aim to finish the game as strong as I started".

The group began its final climb and exit from the park, led by our Mikes crazy Boxer dog Buster who was only near challenged for enthusiasm by his owner. Who in what seemed an instant had scaled the ninety-nine steps and was back encouraging his team with said loyal dog at his side. My day's nemesis was alongside me with his load, his earlier comments now nothing more than a distant memory as my early insecurities of fitness now being replaced by the glow of satisfaction of near completion.

I had already batted off a couple of repeat offers to relieve me of my dual load as my Mike made his third and final lap of the last sector and as I reached the top. I was transported back to my entry into the Triton Inn car park after our Half-Marathon. Looking up through the morning rising sun over his shoulder, breaking through the canopy of the trees there he stood saying more in silence than a thousand words ever could, as he once more doffed his imaginary cap at my efforts.

Unbeknown to any of us at that time, that point as I carried the cans back to the collection of cars and drinks bottles would be the last time, I would complete a Bootcamp with my amazing brother......

9

2 laps of military testing

Switzy is like many other landmarks of areas are a feature point for a diverse group of people, all of which can call it their home for a certain place in their life or regular activity. Even in general conversation I have found that friends and acquaintances from far and wide used the place as a lunchtime fitness run, a place to remember family members who walked equally as loved pets daily through its paths and waters.

This recollection of a circuit that has its origins in a lot of beer but firmly sits as one of the best tests of my stamina I have ever completed.

The two men I took this accompanied challenge from, I met on a stag do from my beloved Norland and the friendship remains to this day twenty-four years later.

These guys were/are and always will be loyal servants of our Crown and armed forces and as such deployments or base would see them away for long periods if not even permanently.

As such when the diaries finally aligned and the obligatory piss up had been dutifully honoured, I was told that this pair were to be completing a quick run to keep their phys in check whilst enjoying this particular set of R&R.

My dual leads for this alien even to me run was Phil "Cushy" Cowen and Andy "Stan" Stamford.

Phil – "Cush" - a square shouldered, stoic servant of the Military Police, proud, dare I say good looking twat with a silver tongue and a nose that make you question his religion and origin. Who had a number of roles in life, from one of the most legendary families in Hull folklore. Who quite simply took that name and made it even better. In Cush what the frame lacked the heart compensated and then some with a power to weight ratio up there with the best of them. Deeply entrenched in the local Rugby League scene never short of helping out via physio duties and if needed pulling a shirt on, a mister in all senses of the word.

Andy – "Stan" – a man of stature in all that he did, still a proud Marine, casting a shadow with both his stature and his abilities. Standing with an engaging smile and banter that saw him literally play the Jester of any group. Respected hugely on and off the field by opposition and peers alike. In fairness one of my true regrets was the lack of time I spent on the field with Stan such was the rating he had from our groups.

As you can see the combination of these titans with a run ahead, my insecurities made for a fair bit of trepidation but also nervous excitement for where I could rate myself alongside them. Top car park was the meeting point and the description did not help with the nerves, two laps of the park then out onto the front along the railway lines to Ferriby and back.

Now the two laps are old hat and muscle memory would not let me down, I had done more sessions on these paths than a fat lad asks for seconds. For me the real nerves were the add on if you will.

Any run along the Humber was fraught with a real natural occurring challenge – the wind. Now being of a certain build and ears that have seen me described at best a wing nut, similarly the FA Cup. Wind is no friend of mine at any time let alone in the face of this challenge. Now the direction of the wind is the great variable of this route as any gust will run along the river, it is only the direction that helps or hinders you.

As we set off in our trio the two laps were completed with no real concerns, maybe a little quick but I was more than up for this run. As we completed and headed up and over the tarmac hill down onto the front were faced with a locked gate. This stood at probably four feet high and with spacing's between the uprights of about a foot and a half, decision pending was jump over and risk falling like a tit or go under and risk my back. Buoyed by my warmed-up bones I bent and went under, this allowed Cush and Stan to pull away a little as they scaled the obstacle as if a wooden bench in a military sports hall.

Upping the pace to regain parity in the group it was evident the wind Gods were shining and a head wind faced us on the outward leg. Meaning of course that I would get a little assistance when fatigue kicked in at the turn. With each stride we took I noted but could not work out that Cush and Stan were talking and asking me questions pretty much constantly. Coupled with this one of the pair would drop a little spurt of pace into the run, not sprint and still within four or five strides but enough to make me change pace. Something I struggled with eternally owing to having two paces – stop and go.

On the turn and with a very welcome favourable wind I again drew up to the varying paced pair and we made it back into my much more familiar surroundings of Switzy, across the park and up the ninety-nine steps and back to the cars. A point at which I had plans to ask a burning question for my two torturers. Almost as if my near exhausted mind was being read, Stan quipped good run that Dunny. Carrying on, "we tested you over and over again and you responded every time". Cush further explained that two of the major factors that disappear in fatigue is the ability to communicate – the questions –

and responding to challenge – the increased pace. I keep this lesson close to my heart in all my coaching and conditioning sessions to this day.

10

Twins with Mummy

More years had passed between the recollection of the memories and with quite some change in this chapter. We move onto a very emotive time for me as we were now parents of the amazing pair that are Madison and Riley, our beautiful twins.

Getting them here was a minor miracle in itself, the conception alone was following two rounds of IVF. Inclusive of a scare that led us to believe that we were losing our baby, only to have a scan that confirmed we were having two babies.

This news alone took us from our near on perfect setting of a two bedroomed, semi-detached, sandwiched between great neighbours. Complete with shared drive, off road garage parking home – the list went on. To a search that pretty much began whilst Shelley was still pregnant and finished with a move to an all too big but perfectly available house that kept us both in area and somewhere near our budget.

A pregnancy that flitted with regularity from serene happiness at the miracle unfolding in my stunning wife's body to panic. Which included an early event of movement courtesy of our eventual daughter and a potential move out of area for the birth of our pair due to their decision to arrive a good 6 weeks prior to due date.

In times of concern we would fear the arrival at all and in times of calm we would afford ourselves a dream or nightmare of the potential configuration when the pair were born.

When the day was upon us and the twins made their bow the two greatest achievements of my life were complete. First out was a beautiful daughter that would give my Mum her princess to spoil and secondly a son that gave my Dad the contentment that our proud family name was defended for another generation at least.

It was following the required move and a recovery from a spell in high dependency unit suffering from pneumonia for our Maddy. That we embarked upon our first family trip around the park that had so many stories told and so many yet to come. As we set off it was with a lot of excitement and obvious nerves about moving our amazing pair who were not even three years old yet. Introducing our pair to terrain that had caused their father so many issues at ages of at least twice over their tender years.

As with many of our first trips we were terribly under prepared in nearly all areas, in fact I reckon looking back at videos and photos of the trip it was only the coats that we got right. A story of typical comparison was a cross town run to pick up bedroom items for the twins that was done with no change bag, milk in fact anything.

The days weather was far from severe in any way but as with the surrounding unless the day was arid dry the conditions underfoot would be wet, which means mud and lots of it. Mummy for some reason decided it was pertinent to wear the whitest coat she could find. Yours truly basked in the knowledge gained over years that I was prepped for any conditions.

Call it genetic, call it nature but clearly as we began our walk around the twins quickly allayed any fear that we had over their potential ability to manage the new surroundings. Moving swiftly from holding Mummy's hand on the descent down the stairs that Daddy had addressed so many times, we swept around the top of the water areas. This section to kids of such a tender year would rightly be thought of as daunting, more than an occasional change in gradient. An option to drop over a set of steps or down a slope follows, then it is a steadier downhill section under a canopy of trees and shadowed by imposing sheer face walls hewn from the chalk of the park's past.

As we moved around, consecutive Gabion style cages formed retaining walls at the base of short and sharp inclines of almost gravel like pieces of chalk that depending on the dryness of the park would be loose or compact. Luckily as the day was damp, we had compact underfoot conditions for what was about to happen. Owing more to a rarely seen foolhardy nature as I lifted the kids on to the first, and more stable of the cages.

The notion in this weird head of mine was that we would each have one of the twins holding our hands walking along the cages akin to all those moments of parents assisting with the adventures along dwarf wall tops giving away the thrill yet keeping the control required by all new parents.

Now I am convinced that even the lowest amount of attention paid to my exploits in this book would serve for you to understand that any plan in this place had a snowball in hells chance of success. As quick as the grasp of our hands took place and the walk began the kids, almost instinctively pulled toward the incline and not along the wall as the romantic plan stated.

Led by Madison - a direction that would carry on for many years to come in vocal and physical nature – the twins took off up the chalk hill. Struck motionless by the split options of watching the kid's ascent or checking that Shelley's heart was still beating. I paused before following the kids up as quickly as humanly possible.

Now I am unsure if anyone has ever been met with a girl still not at her third birthday, scaling an incline and smiling through her dummy, but should you ever share a similar experience please treasure this moment in the way I did as this moment is etched in this gorilla's heart forever.

The wave of emotion and joy was quickly checked by "that" tone from Shelley as her call of OK that will do now. Was the clearest of indicators that it was time to cease this foolish yet delightful moment and return to the more standard family stroll. Never the less with all the memories born from this day, a joyous fact remains that my beautiful pair would undoubtedly follow their Daddy's and of course Uncle's well worked footsteps in enjoying all Switzy has to offer.

So, as the virgin walk of the newest generation of Dunn's was now confined to the past. This very proud father was left only wanting to come back soon, to scribe another memory into the walls of this great playground.

11

Twins with Uncle Mike and Buster

Despite the glorious recollection of our first family trip round Switzy, plus the countless number of escapades enjoyed in the playground. Very few would turn out to have more of an emotional attachment than this particular day.

Prior to the day's proceedings we had been dealt a crushing blow in the family with news that Mike had been diagnosed with cancer of the oesophagus. My brother who at this time was post operation and back with his beloved Fire and Rescue Service based at Clough road as incident support on the engines. One of his major achievements in this role was to revive a lifeless dog – Sunny – following a house fire. An act that would see fame rightly brought upon him through local, national press and with Eamon and Ruth on ITVs This

Morning. A fantastic morning when he was interviewed and delivered himself fantastically well.

When he contacted me and said that he wanted to take the twins around Switzy for, as he put it for some fun. I was aware that as beautiful of an idea this was Mike may well be approaching a stage of some fear that he may not have many of these opportunities remaining. A worry not least endorsed by the concern that this evil had the potential to grab him as it had so many other members of our family.

Meeting on the top car park the day changed from overcast to a stunning summer's day, a meteorological happening that would repeat so many times in events and dates of celebration and remembrance that it felt that he somehow, in life and death, controlled the appearance of the sun.

Not that the young pair required any extra need to be excited in the presence of Uncle Mike but the accompanying Buster; A white Boxer dog that almost mirrored his owner in enthusiasm and love to give, completed that frenzy. A requested picture by our Mike that remains a prize possession was duly completed and into the park we set our course.

In expectation of a steady walk round, some over bearing fussing of Buster our never tiring canine companion and a few memories for the kids to be reminded of were almost instantly blown away.

At the kissing gate entry point, instead of heading straight on and down the steps into the ring of the park, we instead turned left to pick up the every top part of the bowl, which dropped severely to a second level still a good twenty feet above the pathway we eventually wished to be on. Buster blazed a trail as if a prior discussion had taken place between dog and master regarding the day's events. Quickly reporting back on this occasion in almost telepathy to tell Mike that the plan was a goer.

The descent that changed from a meander down the steps had turned into a scramble that drew shrieks of excitement from Maddy and Riley, the latter of which was still not confident but in the presence of his Uncle showed bravery beyond anything displayed before. In a nod to our family trip months previous I was pretty certain that the very first assault on the hills of the park. The route would have drawn the concern rather than enjoyment of the twin's excitement had the attendees been different, before the day had even got off the ground.

Luckily the day was ours and I like to believe that there was a kind of allowance being subconsciously sent by Shelley for us all to enjoy this special time, in a way brothers or indeed any siblings should.

This type of start and smiles across all faces was all Mike needed to carry this approach on unchecked. In what seemed to be a timeless period in which we covered every ascent, descent, set of stairs and thanks to Buster was made wet from the water areas on the bottom of the park.

Obligatory attempts at entertaining the kids by skimming the smoother off shoots of the chalk was met with further shrill approval by the twins. Also, when two young children see the adults that they already hold in such high regard throwing stones into the drink there is only one follow on that is destined to happen. With playful charm again and again and again the pair bent down to retrieve anything bearing a resemblance to what we were skimming with and proceeded to plonk them in the water. This time belly laughs replacing the shrill responses but with no less energy.

As the day was drawing to a close and we were exiting the park waves of emotion could no longer be hidden as we took a look at each other in a moment of understanding that neither wanted to admit. But this had the genuine potential to be the last time we would be active together as Father, Brother, Uncle and the twins. This was hard but also a feeling that would steel us to finish on a high – quite literally – as a random swing was spotted. Throwing up those shared memories of my first time in the playground. Now clearly even a carefree pair of brothers were not about to endanger this beautiful pair the way I had been many moons ago but, by the same token we were not about to give up the opportunity of this contraption of joy. Following on in shifts long enough to have a moment to treasure but not too long as to test the patience of our young companions for the day, we threw ourselves back many years to kids on a swing – crude in design, untested, yet giving off a magnetism that would always draw us in.

We finished on the latterly nick named Uncle Mikes steps and into the car park to our respective cars that signaled the end of a very emotional day in our church.

Now in all the years since the twins have had the uncanny ability to orate their own memories of keys times and places, they have recalled this day with unerring accuracy. This was a point of emotive confusion for Shelley and myself when I looked back at the age our twins would have been at the time of this event. An age which surely confirmed that they could never have actual memory of this, we put it down to the fact that we never shy from discussions with our pair in respect of our Mike. This is done irrespective of how upsetting they can be, ensuring details are recalled at whatever the twins request is.

What I can say beyond doubt is that Shelley and myself expand the memories our twins have of that time which lends itself to being the more dominant contributor of their recollection. Whatever the reason, I do not care for the finer detail and nor do my kids when they smile in its presence. A smile that is both infectious and pure.

As I sat that night after putting the twins down, having contemplated but decided against filling Shelley in on the day's movements. Emotion hit me savagely as in a time of appointments and commitments overtaking family matters, that this would indeed be the last time we spent time together actively.

12

Scouting for girls and a lot of tears

"Son go and get your Mum", 0745hrs, 24th April 2012.

The year of years a home Olympics to be lauded, our Majesties Diamond Jubilee to be celebrated. A feel-good period for our great nation would surely have no setbacks would it?

Unfortunately for our family this was never going to be a time to rejoice, having watched our Son, Brother, Uncle and best friend, fight with all his might the evil of cancer. We had been made aware that the invasion to the purest of bodies was now a terminal occupant.

Topping out at fourteen stones at his best and weighing in at several different points dependent on which event / challenge was in that sector of his career. This embodiment of inspiration had been confined to his house for some time now. His weight and look were one now I did want to estimate or see but a hand forced by the morbid sense of seeing a job through. As devastating as this job was to be, I wanted to be in his presence in life the day before. Alas not to be on the day my brother left this earth a worse place for not having him in it.

For those of that have more in-depth knowledge of yours truly my nation is held in the highest of regard. The day before the passing of this great saw me attend work and attend my constant in prison life, the Seg.

No need to check detail in them days, no need for a spot at the Wailing Wall. Self-rostering ruled on the good ship Everthorpe in all its glory. A clarity of job, shift, even leave and potential stitch ups was yours a month in advance. This day, St Georges day was a time that I had packed gym bag with a particularly favourite England shirt. The plan being to display in my nod to our Dragon slaying patron saint, in all its splendour in the prison cardio area.

Imagine if you would the disappointment of finding out on entry to the Seg that not only where we short of a dinner patrol, but I was lowest on hours in that month so it was my "honour" to complete said duty.

Out of nowhere appeared a guest gaffer – in short this was more a fucking hindrance, then leader in a well-run Seg or any help. I can however confirm emotionally and ever thankfully that this man, Mr. Andrew Lee arrived in a similar predicament as myself in respect of hours deficit. "Here Dunny you like the Gym, why don't you let me do your dinner cover and you get the back of yer neck wet?" An offer that would change the last memory of my brother in a way that I hope I do justice with my words here.

Brutally in the preceding week I had taken time off to spend whatever period was available at my brothers' home in Kingscroft Drive, Welton. On one of these days I had gone off to make a brew for the two of us when his amazing wife Katie had returned home. In adjusting the number and amount of water in the kettle to change the order from two to three brews, Katie had got upstairs and was conversing with my brother who had asked a question that was a dagger to my heart.

"Why is our kid in civvies every time he comes around now?" a query that inferred that I had put my life on hold for the inevitable end, the hardest part was he was absolutely right.

Dunn's have an annoying habit of being that way.

Wracked with overcoming emotion I made a loud artificial noise as went up the first set of town house stairs onto the living level with said brews. The conversation had returned back to more magnolia of trivial matters – shopping, cars etc. Attempts by myself to continue ensued but the elephant in the room was as obvious as the amount of medication that was on his table next to his sofa. Finishing my drink, I made my excuses to leave and fought with my tears until I was safely in my car and back on the A63. A drive that I have no recollection of how I completed at that point and home.

At that point my decision was made to return to work, even though mentally in no fit state I had to try and restore some order to this emotional explosion I was enduring.

That return date was that Monday, the penultimate day of my brothers' life and the day I had in avertedly been given a free pass to enjoy a bonus gym session.

The mornings movements on the morning of St George's day passed me by and before I appeared to have blinked it was dinner hour. With gym bag in hand I had key in lock on my way to my session. What happened next, I have no explanation for and make no attempt any more to do so. I dropped my gym bag, walked to the gate and left for my brother's house. On my way I saw the Principal Officer in charge of the daily gave a brief of what I was doing (the establishment was more than aware of the family's situation – my Dad also worked at the prison). No histrionics with his response, just "see you when you get back".

I drove through the lions at the end of the drive on my way to a house that for the first time since Mike and Katie moved in, I did not know the reception that would await.

On seemingly empty roads I drove and upon arrival at the home I had been beaten by my Dad who was not tied to leaving by the dinnertime roll. He was already in position on a chair next to my brother's bed thumbing through a book – Lance Armstrong, images of a champion. On my entry to the room dressed in full prison uniform, I brushed past his now oversized dressing gown that was over the door of his room I was invited to take the seat where my Dad was sat. Almost simultaneously my brother requested that my Dad left the room which with a quip of charming – or words to that effect, obliged. I moved to peruse the book left by my Dad and flicked through the pictures painfully aware that a need for a poignant talk was in the air.

As my brother beckoned me over, we shared a moment that was almost rendered impossible by that day's potential events.

Details of our discussion will remain between us as it was a moment in which he shared his deepest wants and fears and we told each other we loved each other for what turned out to be the last time.

For some reason, maybe a desperate attempt to regain a long since lost composure, I returned to the book before making my excuses of a necessary return to work. A just about tearless embrace with Katie I made the return journey to the lions.

Would I be able to recall whether I broke a speed limit, drove through a red light, ignored an obvious give way point, not a chance? In fact, the only repeating thought I had through this haze was that I needed some regularity to a period of time. This was a period which felt like I was looking through a camera lens that was covered in Vaseline.

I of course found that in my Seg and worked the remainder of my shift despite a well-deserved dressing down from said Principal Officer. Who questioned, as caringly as he could why I had returned.

That journey back, that morning, to Kingscroft Drive was completed in a knowing silence that the time had come. When we arrived and went into my brothers' room he lay peacefully, the book still on the floor and in mercy the pain was over for Mike and about to manifest in so many ways across our family.

As more members of the family arrived the gravity of the situation hit us all, obligatory drinks were made – well how else were a house full of proud Brits going to face this horrendous time without a brew. The calls to the undertakers, medical support and all were completed.

This was my time to leave and make my way to a place that I needed to start my process. Now I read somewhere that at a time such as this being alone is the worst place to be and not telling people where you are arguably worse.

With a mantra of abiding by rules and respecting order my decisions at this point were, probably emotively driven but wholly out of character. Should a search party have ever been needed at that point in time I think Messrs. Poirot, Columbo, Holmes and even Drebin could have had a day off as I was only going to be in one place – Switzy.

Following a call to Shelley to confirm the expected news and one to the Prison, off I set to attend that place. At this point I wish I could share that the memorable memory of a song for the ages playing on the radio or a nod to his favourite films. Sadly, no it was Scouting for girls with this ain't a love song that stuck at this point.

Parking up and walking toward the steps I passed the kissing gate and my legs felt akin to leaving a ride at Hull Fair. Owed in no small part to the culmination of the events of the last 48 hours.

Almost staggering now, I made it to the bench at the top of the 99 steps, slumped and lost control of most of my facial/emotional responses. This is a place of immense activity as alluded to earlier and what the dog walkers and fitness enthusiasts must have thought I have no idea and honestly did not care.

As I came around, thoughts and functions returning I took off for a walk and a chat with my now departed hero. The content of this I will never recall but even at that early point in grief my scrambled thought process was dominated by one factor.

What if I carried on to the gym that 23rd April, would I have ever seen my brother again? Most importantly to me would we have finished on the terms that felt so sour due to his concerns the Friday before?

Thanks to a fellow warder and his equal inability to keep his own hour's right, plus that feeling that overcame me at the back doors of my Seg. This remains an eventuality that I will never have to ponder. More importantly than all of this my crumb of comfort through my darkest of days, is I believe that my brother held on to speak one last time to me.

13

Snowy on the scene

Our family was moving on well, twins a solid year into schooling, Shelley and myself holding good position in our respective careers. Alongside this, slowly but surely the house we bought from necessity was being transformed into a home we were rightly proud of. Big work was courtesy of a network of trades and skills in both family and friendship circles and the minors or less technical work by Shelley and myself.

Next on the horizon for team Dunny was the inevitable pet to complete our set. So, studies were undertaken and several viewed by the power of internet. A decision was made that a Cocker Spaniel was to be our canine companion. Female was the advice as they know their place in the hierarchy – well that turned out to be complete bollocks but anyway on with rest!!

A trip to Hatfield to "have a look!" of course turned into a commitment to buy. Thanks in no small part to when the litter was released into our excited family's presence one in particular pup decided to avoid the strokes and belly rubs the other were enjoying choosing instead to sneak round my back and take hold of my trainer socks in her teeth. If love at first sight could be adjusted to bite this canine stole our hearts in a way that only dogs can.

The naming of our pup took a while as we searched for a neutral name following the female recruitment policy that was in place and eventually Snowy was declared.

If awaiting the collection day took a long time the time taken to take her on a "real" walk seemed never ending. You see controlled walks to Mappleton – wash of the seawater takes away the dangers of infection apparently – are all well and good. Whilst also serving as a fantastic option on a long summer's day but Switzy is where I wanted to be at with my new mate.

By nature, the breed is inquisitive but famed for its returning nature, her runs took an almost circular motion when out on local fields. We built confidence steadily to finally let her off in my playground.

A whistle developed, confidence in her listening to instruction and a good number of times off the lead completed prep for our maiden run.

Almost instinctively Snowy set off with abandon that the breed has. Yet true to character stopped and checked for allowance on the rapid exploration of this amazing playground. One that had engaged, entertained, supported and conditioned her family for years and now was doing similar for her.

Now luckily for the under prepared owner – see all previous chapters! – we did not introduce Snowy to the water area on the first few times around Switzy but once we did the game had changed forever. A throwaway comment from a dog owner at work came unbelievably true when I steadily lobbed Snowy's ball toward the drink; Once a spaniel hits the water you will never get it out.

Cautiously Snowy tiptoed into the drink and retrieved her ball and with each subsequent throw the distance increased. Then arrived the excited anticipation from the mutt for the next throw and allowance to get wet through.

As such the prep for a walk had gone from lead, ball and poo bags to include towels, car covers. Latterly through bitter experience any type of makeshift block to stop her climbing through from the boot to decorate my car with whatever we hadn't cleaned off her.

My only issue now was to navigate a route that kept her out of the bleeding water long enough to do the business we take her out to do…….

14

The Mighty Comets

A straightforward nod to all of my history in this park is the origin of the next offering in this book.

When like myself you are thrown into coaching at any age or experience you clamber, scrap and dig deep in to your very soul for a reference point. A point that helps you through a dark moment, that moment when all your options are exhausted. When even the simplest of drills left for you by your co-coach are not making any sense.

I have taught many different sports and arts in my time but due to a moment of my mouth getting me in trouble; Never a long search to find examples to be fair! I found myself assistant coach of my boy's football team.

Now if the rather cynical opinion of a coach or teacher is one of "if you can't do – teach" I have always had in my pocket the counter given to me by one of the bluntest forces I have ever met in life, Mr. Gary Scott. Who once said "it's not about being the best – its knowing how to be". As such the very DNA of this approach was needed when I took my boy to his new found passion of football.

There are many bruised shin, calf and thigh from Everthorpe Gym that bear testament to my lack of footballing ability, knowing how to was my only hope. Six months of watching and seeing assistants come and go and the enthusiasm of our boys' coach physically dwindle as he tried to juggle all tasks needed in this role.

Adam, who is a Polish national living in the Kings Town of Hull with an eventual plan to be full time football coach but in the instance to gain a full-time contract in warehousing. With his wife and two children fully engaged in the English culture of work and education Adam was somewhat of a shining example to other "foreigners" in our town. In short already a man I seriously wanted to help.

So, when I saw one day, that Adam looked more tired than usual I took off to collect some cones for him and offer my assistance. An instant, if nervy acceptance was offered and born that Saturday morning was a relationship that although strange, works very well. Would I ever see myself in a coaching partnership with a man that has English as a second language, involved in a sport I have no experience in? Despite the all too obvious barriers present in this partnership has blossomed ever since. I have, unsurprisingly to those who know me well been a lone wolf with very few exceptions. These times are when I have a partner so different from me the opposites attract, potential matures and we find a way to get on for the better of our charges at the time.

Adam is clearly this person – maybe the language barrier that exists – which leads Adam to speak in a much more basic, agricultural way if you will. A nature and manner which knits with how I converse. Whatever the reason we have it right for the most important people in this equation which is the lads we coach.

What was quickly ascertained was with a bit of luck and creative detailing our shifts would rarely clash to a point when one of us was not there. Thankfully to old banana feet here would have both of us in tow. Weirdly game days were easier in Adams absence, but inevitably the day was due when I would have to look after our Mighty Comets as a solo coach.

I attempted a session planner which was in effect a diluted version of Adams. Which I ran for the first few sessions under my tutelage. Paired with attempted cross over drills from my Rugby League which were practically sound but due to my nerves lacked a fun element.

A quick text ahead of my next session to Adam requesting permission to take not only his son Filip but the rest of our team into the depths of country park and obviously my playground. Adam accepted and a change in venue on the teams Facebook page soon had a string of messages of not real concern. They were although certainly requiring some convincing. Not least trusting this gruff, skin headed lump that had only been part of the club for 6 months to take their lads around a country park.

So, my points of reference tested I went back to my amazing fathers offering at all of his Karate teaching in an open offer to all parents to not just to observe; He would also couple this with joining in with the session which was a huge turning point and set the scene perfectly.

My instructions were simple, old clothes and a cover for your car to collect your child in; Oh and obviously telling people where we wanted them. Now even in having to explain what this place is and what beauties it holds did not dampen my enthusiasm of taking these lads around my church.

The day was cold, wet and cold and I had dressed appropriately as had my lad and my concerns were the dress of the rest of the team. Now I needn't had worried as all lads were layered but many of the parents had a lot to be concerned. Namely as the old clothing request had been completely ignored as lads had a range of football kits atop their warm clothing. Which for detail were inclusive of but not exhaustive to, two sets of white Manchester United shorts and a Real Madrid Ronaldo full kit resplendently white but not right for this session.

Unabashed by the wardrobe of the lads and post completion of an inspirational idea on the way to the session. I decided I would send a non-partaking parent for a round of hot sandwiches' that would serve as a warmer and a moment for all the lads to share after the mud and leaves. It was high time we set about our runaround.

Our entry point was the concrete steps and we descended with no real concerns and over the railway sleepers we had soon passed.

As we wrapped around the sharp right hand and first semi obstructing tree, I sent the lads up its chalky surround, think about 12 feet of climbing with a mid-level of incline. What followed seemed as if this group of lads were playing out all of my experiences and nerves within five minutes of commencement. This spectrum of lads now through this obstruction and together under a copse of trees. An area that would a couple of months earlier be giving a canopy that would block out the larger amounts of any weather in the general Hessle area. What was staring back from these gathered eyes was a heady mix of nerves, excitement and complete delirium at these surroundings. A simple adjustment of route and the group was united at least in approach if not climbing ability.

    Curiosity of how much work I could get out of the lads had me start my Strava, and as we took a run to the next climb, I knew a fair distance was already been covered. My charges were paired off to aid with confidence, which is as dangerous of a slave as it is a master. Those delirious at the opportunity of climbing uphill and down dale were as, if not more dangerous than a player mirroring that young Matt Dunn on his first expedition round a 1980's Switzy.

With the best planning in the world for varying abilities at some point and inevitable slip or trip was due, that did not take long as before hitting the track that heads toward the water area our boys headed up an incline that was a lot more mud than chalk. Although not a face over apex fall many of the Mighty Comets had to take the evasive action of sliding on their backsides; Not the preferred option when wearing the white shorts of the North Wests Red Devils or Spain's capital dwelling Galactico's Real Madrid. As the ground in near black stains on the rear of the shorts confirmed.

Now alongside a day of fun in the area which I know so well and would never be flustered. Came a hope that under the guise of mud, leaves and climbing I would instill a new level of fitness in our lads that is all too obvious to them in on field sessions. So, a longer run cunningly hidden behind some range of moment drills ended when we got to an incline that would take us to a plateau of real discovery for the lads. This incline had two options for ascent and it was time to let them have their head and attack the way they saw fit, with an obvious caveat of once up they were to work round and help until all the team was on the same level. To my amazement, I should not have thought any less of them, systematically every player was assisted to the top – with even more damage to the kit of our white clad players! Until we had only one challenge left before the long run back to the car park, which of course was the descent back to the track down below.

In no way whatsoever was this as united or graceful as the ascent but we all made it and we set off for the car park and the sandwich shop bounty that awaited. The parents were awaiting some nervously others happy that I had tired their offspring for an hour. As my buttie running parent presented the treats for the lads I remain to this day unaware of how they actually ate their sandwich as they excitedly recalled their favoured points of spills and thrills of the last hour. Not only had this served to remove any remaining barriers and secure the trust of the players and parent's alike. It had given me the confidence that in my oldest and dearest go to place I had the perfect venue to unite players and parents alike.

This ritual continues to the date of writing this as does the progression of our fantastic group, I hope in no small part to these days and the only variants are the level of hangover displayed by the parents and the type of treat that awaits the end of our session. Ice cream for summer and Butties for colder times.

15

Park run chasing the boy

One of the major shifts in the footfall of Switzy recently and in its history to be fair, is the inception of the Humber Bridge Parkrun. For anyone alien to this marvelous movement; A now worldwide network of clubs and their willing volunteers organise, plan, marshall and co-ordinate a five-kilometer run starting at 0900hrs every Saturday morning.

In a place that you have already seen catalogued herein that has as diverse as large population of users organising such an event is a task that I would want little to do with, even with my knowledge of layout.

The inclines and natural loops of the park – which are completed 3 times in all, make it a fantastic hybrid of quick track and off-road underfoot conditions. Couple this with the seasonal changing of weather and the protection from the fluid canopy of the trees and their leaves. You can easily see the attraction of this venue to complete your weekly 5k.

One of these volunteers who arrive at least an hour prior to the safety talk and call to begin at 0900hrs is my beautiful wife Shelley. Thanklessly apart from fellow willing helpers she arrives to divvy up tickets, scanning, marking out direction signs through to donning the obligatory hi vis vests and stand at potentially confusing sections to unsure runners. The weekly safety briefing must be a task that grates on even the announcer but like all great movements a person takes this role on with gusto. Delivering with style the updated hazards to be aware of. Fallen trees, puddles that had become ponds that require navigation and of course the permanent threat of the steps that must be avoided at all costs. After and only after it is time to set the runners, joggers, walkers and those not sure until they have completed a lap how they will complete the course.

Mrs. Dunn is a proud rep of the City of Hull running club and as such likes to complete the 5k infrequently yet also has a time she likes to keep to. This is irrespective of underfoot or overhead conditions and it was after she had run with our beautiful pair on one occasion – they had attended to help but wanted to run instead. That our first Father / Son challenge was born.

The simple almost throw away comment from Mrs. Dunn was in regard to the twin's effort on the run. Namely Maddy' attempts at staying below her threshold for breathing difficulties following her asthma diagnosis post pneumonia and Riley's pace that would have been even better if he wasn't talking all the time. The pride of my daughter's physical efforts in my church probably meant more than anything at this point as my sons' athletic ability was as obvious as his late uncle; Even in these young years. It was, however the last line of the quote by Mrs. Dunn that hit home and stoked memories of my military mates testing system.

Clearly without an ability to turn down a challenge I set the date to fit in with shifts at work. Also ensured our comets training would not be affected by a later start and planned to test this out for myself. On the day, which even by Switz's standard had a challenge weather wise I decided on a compression top under my yellow "Mile for Mike" T-shirt. Uncovering that despite two layers of quality fabric were doing little to hide the lack of shape I was in.

Uninterested in trivialities such as my back and at least one of my knees was now one injury from full reconstruction I still wanted to complete the 3 laps in my mean time of 30 minutes. With the boy stood next to me in dry but cold conditions in more of his Manchester United kit. He was already gassing with his subject matter as random as the group that we stood in was. The staple beginnings to the run were completed inclusive of announcements of milestone runs and introductions of how far afield the runners were from. Scotland and Devon were two of the families running on this day, proving that you really can just turn up with your barcode and run in most towns and cities in the UK. We set off.

Now the field contains many serious runners who are getting their splits in – whatever that means – and those who are at the very start of their running journey with literally everything else in between. Away from the start and onto the first incline up the tarmac incline that has caused me such dread down my years. Sees a hell of a lot of jockeying for position and placing's.

This was never the case for me and the lad as we settled in to a steady stride which quickly reminded me that I had overdone it with the compression top. Completing the incline section of the first lap and looped back into the open green to receive well intended support from the volunteers. Mrs. Dunn front and centre of this group more for the lad I am sure but I will take any encouragement. Now the issue of encyclopedic knowledge of a place is that when completing laps of it under someone else's organisation is that dominantly you can be caught up in group pacing. In addition due to the fact that you know exactly what you have left to do, can slow your pace. Every incline, decline, long section so this in mind it is warming that support is given.

The start is at best, through the third lap of both running and listening to the continuous chatter of my boy and days running partner. Providing the point when the runners of decent standard pass you and are not seen again unless you arrive at the start line for next week's run. Runners are a strange breed; in fact, they are just weird. But I digress from the boy that had not only dragged me round in an acceptable 30 minutes he had talked and encouraged me throughout. I believe a high five was still down with the kids at the time so we shared this after recording our times. A quick kiss with Mrs. Dunn and it was time to transition from chasing the boy in Switzy to coaching him at football.

It was a difficult call that day which part of the morning had given more pride, but due to my connections with the place Parkrun just gets the nod.

16

The Body with a history

At some point with the regularity of a person's visits to an area there will be a time when a catalogue of emotion, humour, joy, fear and discovery a more sinister visit happens. Many reports of such a discovery are underpinned with a detail of jogger / dog walker finds……

That find was in a life changing way for me a man hung by the neck in the lay of the chalk face, but this find was to explode in involvement in a way I could not have imagined. This record of my innocent attempt to "awaken a slumbering man" provides unintentional proof of my natural tendency to digress in storytelling.

The day in March 2017 started as structured as any rest or late shift begun in the complex dovetailing world of my amazing wife and me.

Kids readied for school; dog readied for a walk all three bundled in the car then the short hop round Gisburn for a quick shuffle around the slower walkers into the playground. A shout across said area for my twin terrors to give Daddy a cuddle before they entered the school.

I would always wait until I saw the back of my daughter's locks pass the teacher on door duty before departing. Next a dash back to the car for the longer drive to Switzy to give Snowy her essential daily exercise.

Park up in top car park this time and down the now perma-named Uncle Mikes steps and a sharp right – avoiding the water area to keep Snowy dry and have her ablutions was today to have more complex eventualities. Over the hump which is the first blind spot that causes a few nerves as we need to avoid the irregular path of a

Dalmatian that took a particular dislike to my canine best friend. This section clear and the first few of innumerable ball throws for my ever-willing cocker to chase completed I found a calm that was about to explode into an ordeal that I never imagined. My wag tailed companion into her stride, myself running through hypothetical issues at work. An approach that seemed to prepare for the late or indeed any shift I was walking into presenting that all on the surface was "sweet".

As I looked around at the early budding trees that accompanied the evergreen bushes, I saw a man laid against the incline of the chalk prostrate with eyes closed. A mix of disgust at why someone would be in this state in my park, fueled by my protective feelings towards the place. Quickly joining this cocktail was growing concern at the wellbeing of this man as I called out in an attempt to rouse.

"Time to wake up pal" was repeated a couple of times as I swung another boot at Snowys ball and she scuttled off in pursuit. Now not of quiet voice, monotone yes; quiet, no I expected a reaction. By the third attempt a stiffness hit my spine that would be unfortunately matched by the man as I approached. A sixth sense moment as the realisation dawned that I had found a body. On approach what I found was a man eyes bulging, red in faced and more crimson in the visible area of the neck. The face was not fully visible as a scarf covered this.

I now physically attempted to gain a response from the man which again proved fruitless, wetting the back of my hand to gauge breath. I followed by lowering my ear to the oronasal area whilst looking down the torso to see if any rise and fall of the chest was visible. I was now close to belief that this is a body rather than a man not responding.

Retracting from close proximity I investigated the neck again to see the scarf was indeed a snood style scarf that he had fashioned into a figure of eight loop. Withdrawing a little further I observed that the scarf was in fact hooked over a sapling, sadly snapped in the grim act that had taken place at an as yet unknown time. I moved to retrieve my mobile and ring in the find. On reporting of the detail of the find and the nature of suspension, the responder strangely enquired – it must be on an algorithm – whether I had a knife to cut the makeshift noose. Answering no, the next instruction made much more sense in regard to asking a fellow passerby to assist with the release from the noose. I managed to commandeer a fellow dog walker to lift the man from his suspension over the sheared sapling and to a rest position. The lady who offered assistance then departed and remains a regret that I did not take more details of her to check on her well-being following this gruesome action we had completed in unison.

As relief from suspension happened the man due to the incline he lay against, slipped to a flatter area by means of gravity. At rest point I rejoined my call to the emergency services on loudspeaker. "I now need you to complete chest compressions until the ambulance responder arrives" was the orderly interaction. I duly obliged and the only further interactions from the call handler was her enquiries whether the man had drawn breath. Added to this was a request that I attempt mouth to mouth, I politely refused this request and continued fruitless CPR. Soon and gladly I heard the sirens of an emergency response. This span of time lasted from later coroner's report from the call over fourteen minutes on chest compressions that left me physically exhausted. The emotional side was nowhere near entering the day's events yet.

My relief was quickly converted to concern for others as the attending ambulance responder, clearly in absence of any local area knowledge. Her attempts to aid as quickly as possible did not respect the underfoot conditions of Switzy and fell heavily, response bag flying one way and herself another. This if any was the best opportunity present, to leave my clearly pointless chest compressions and help her with the bag.

As this lovely lady, embarrassed by her tumble called in the death, she caringly enquired as to my profession to which I responded Prison Service, "I thought so love", The now more relaxed tone filled response, don't usually get details and that amount of calm on the call we get travelling to this kind of job.

Practicalities were now required with the police on scene; being able to account for my movements prior to finding the now confirmed body, what I was to be doing over the next 24 hours and of course the obligatory statement. Notwithstanding a future date at the Coroners court for me to endure. Now as a Prison Officer it is almost an occupational hazard that you will have a trip to the Coroners side of the courts building in Hull. But an almost voluntary appointment is pretty much considered a major error in judgement or at best an unfortunate event. Mine was probably both.

Somewhat concerningly as I finished my chat with the responding officers I was cast aside, left to my own devices to carry on with my walk. Happy in one sense that this was new to me I was very concerned at the lack of what has become to be known as aftercare. Walking around the park in a haze, a few major thoughts consumed me – this has fucked my schedule up as I now have no time to prep a meal for my family. How will I recall any of this when faced by the police interviewers but probably most bothersome was the time of the discovery. You see with the level of knowledge regulars of Switzy have, there is little chance if any, that the footfall of visitors to this place. Considering their almost OCD level of route followed, that no-one would have seen this man possibly at a time that CPR may have revived him.

One of those three concerns was allayed with a phone call to man who in our short time of being muckers had my back as I had his without question Mr. Chris Hill. I rang him dictated my account, he wrote it down, screenshotted it back to give a little structure back to a truly random day.

On my return to my home I bagged up my clothing in readiness for the inevitable visit from the police, prepped a very quick Tuna Pasta bake and donned my uniform before setting off to the prison. To this day justifying my attendance at work remains impossible. In confusion I arrived and headed to my workstation. The route taken saw me encounter the usually engaging resident Police Liaison Officer, whom I accosted for advice on how to deal with the upcoming interview which at the time I had no idea what would happen. His unusually short response was Matty you have nothing to be concerned about but there is a lot more to this.

This did not help my concerns but did allay the second of my fears / concerns from the day. On arrival at my desk one of the elders of our fine establishment – Jim Walker - took one look at me and took me into a side office. I spewed out all details I could recall and aside from a what the fuck are you doing here, Jim requested the attendance of our manager. This led to me being promptly walked off site as quite rightly I was in no fit state to perform any duties.

My return home coincided with a visit from the police – much more supportive this time around. Who confirmed the timing of death was early hours of the morning and exonerating me from any concern. A passing compliment of preparation of my clothing for evidential purposes quickly led to the formality of the statement and our business was complete.

The remaining two flies in the ointment of this story fall into two parts, one of which breaches data loss protocol in my workplace. The other was the father of the man found deceased had been a very close workmate at engineering firm Broadys of my father and my immovable support on the day of the inquest.

As morose as this day was thanks to my effervescent dog and her clear discord at having the primary part of her daily exercise interrupted by this unfortunate incident. A memory was etched that brings a smile at any recollection of this day. As I placed myself alongside the prostrate man and followed the rhythm of the Bee Gees Staying Alive. My unimpressed pup came alongside me and dropped her ball adjacent to the body and expectantly sat for the object be thrown for her. Causing on a number of occasions a pause in the compressions to hurl the ball as far as I could. Luckily a dog walker passing by and seeing my activity stepped in to give some at least temporary relief for myself and entertainment for Snowy.

17

A Sailor, a Dog, a Ferret & a deck of cards

"Deck of cards – 52 cards, 4 suits, transition in to 4 sets of exercises press ups, dips, jacks, burpees etc. performed in numbers as dictated by the shuffled deck with a form of active rest in between each set. 2 jokers in for fun and/or an opportunity for rest – old school version of having a personal trainer"

A long time had passed since my last attendance at a Bootcamp but what I had picked up on my fleeting chats and half sessions with these amazing people that were keeping my brothers' name and ethics going. Was that John – commander in chief of the session now – had, following a painstaking campaign with the Humber Bridge Board gained residency status for the original and best of our towns Bootcamp's.

I had of course made my excuses several times for the reasons my attendance being too sporadic to make it worthwhile to give my commitment. This as all of my protestations to his wonderful group was ignored and I was invited "as and when". It was one of these sessions that one of the biggest compliments to my efforts was paid, whilst completing a tyre pull and finishing as described "like a train" one of the new participants said "I never met your brother, but the effort that lives on in you. Adding the way people speak of him mean he must have been a legend"

Back at the madhouse I was relaying this story in the company of Paul "Dog" Parker (he who scored the last try at the Boulevard). To this day I neither have knowledge or want to know the origin of this nickname - when he said I fancy a session round there.

Without the infrastructure of the newly homed Bootcamp my intention was to go old school and treat Mr. Parker to a game of cards with a shuttle run in-between. I completed a dry run and was happy with the layout and length of the session. By the time Mr. Parker had picked me up for the first of several sessions we already had interest from Mr. Smith (naval officer of the highest regard in my eyes, who bears the brunt of several of my moods and banter) and Mr. Ferrand (a man whose operational career that was cruelly cut short by an injury caused by an idiotic decision) and is affectionately known as Ferret to all that know him.

The devils of detail and weekend on and off starved us of the consistent attendance of all four of us but when these worlds collided a friendship was formed like few others I have enjoyed in my life. In exhaustion and fatigue come a truth, an honesty that comes from very few other environments. We covered the serious subjects of my Yo-yo promotions and accompanying stress levels. Our Sailors new found love and plans for cohabitation, leading to the pitter-patter of tiny feet. The Dogs transition from a fool's gold promise on residential Supervising Officer to the sanctum of Offender Management. Yet the most major of all the continuing events was the claim of our mucker the Ferret. Who was nearing a payout for his injuries that would lead to a life changing emigration to the land of boomerangs and surfboards.

Interspersed with a weekly offer to join the Bootcamp that was beginning atop the bowl of Switzy whilst we set about our variations of the 52 exercises and varying runs that gave the active rest. We naturally had planned the session so we would politely decline stating our lack of regularity as an oxymoronic regular excuse.

This of course had no dampening effect on the enthusiasm or encouragement as the two groups crossed paths.

For this detail poignantly, we recall the final session as a quartet triggered by the decision of our man to sell up, rent out and cut ties in order to try a new life. The gathered opinion of three of our foursome was that aside from jealousy we knew no-one of our group was better placed to give this a bash.

Previously given respect to our sailor was increased as he organised in conjunction with Mr. Parker a post session breakfast at the Home Farm Hotel, obviously after checking it had a grass eating option.

The training about to be undertaken was not diluted in any way, even given the fact Ferret was completing his own "farewell tour" that probably left his knees in tatters but on we went. Our sailor resplendent in his

Navy veterans T-shirt had long since seen his own stress relief become a lot more manual, The Dog was getting used to "cake – well just because" and yours truly was finally getting to grips with his latest promotion, even if our sailor was about to steal his job.

Despite the fatigue of our leading man we completed an hour based at the most open and green area of Switzy using a decent run off to the right that had seven steps leading to a varyingly filled small water area, due to the infamous Hessle water table. The hour was intense in effort and content coupled with weather that from the early morning frost had opened out into stunning sunshine. Adding in the obligatory sight of the run past of John and the Bootcamp regulars.

In conclusion and despite some apparently poor clothing choices by myself we paused for a few photos for posterity of this moment. The short trip to our refuel station; Home Farm, followed and we were soon sat on our pre-booked table. Emotions ran high as did nerves at our version of the last supper.

Following an order that would have satisfied double the numbers in attendance and several hot and cold drinks, we finished up and made our way into the morning. With knowledge that despite our man's protestation otherwise, this was highly likely to be the last time we saw him on our shores.

18

Christmas week nights and then sunshine

The dates had been confirmed and that greatest of all threats on a rolling detail had come true. It was my turn to do Christmas weeks in charge of the now sprawling establishment that I have made my home for the last 13 years, HMP Humber.

Even in the most modern of times those that sit above you in the hierarchy are men and women that have progressed through all the ranks our service has to offer. People who know all the pitfalls and trepidation of any set of nights let alone the nightmare that is Christmas week.

In the weekly operations meeting, the subject of who is doing "that" week came up and my name was banded about almost as if the gallows awaited. Swiftly followed was my own Governor's quotation of the year that he did his set. In these conversations there are detail that confirm that so far apart are the likelihood of a set of yuletide nights. Whether this be that through the size of the group, crazy volunteers who apparently don't mind – you are likely to do very few sets ever in your career. If luck favours you on your promotion pathway you may never get "that" set.

Now in what was a very moving moment several of our at times, completely dysfunctional group had started to get at least up to Christmas Eve covered. In an offering so that I could spend some invaluable family time with my amazing lot. Front and centre of this were Mr. Leach, Micklethwaite and Bryan fully supported by Gov Mitcheson. They duly delivered and I could plan my week with a home Christmas dinner and family time inclusive of our family photo in at least a state of being awake.

On my attendance for work on Christmas night the establishment was creaking under the weight of complimentary chocolates, shortbread and every other type of snack food that could have been handed out. Or indeed brought in to be transported around the footprint of two conjoined establishments that were finally working in something like a settled state.

This amount of surplus food rendered my fruit, houmous, crackers, mackerel and flavoured rice offerings pretty redundant for some very simple reasons.

One of the major jobs of any in charge manager is to visit every area of the nick and check on his charges and documentation. With several of these to do the likelihood of not approaching type 2 diabetes by the early hours of Boxing day were slim to none.

The support grades that at times heroically staff all but one of the residential units as well as the critical comms post, were already dispersing to their posts with the escorting staff. As I took my handover from the late shift nothing really was brewing behind the walls.

Should this have been the case in the remainder of the week's nights I was in good stead if not in possession of the best of numbers of staff. I had more than enough quality to assist me through any waters.

The week passed steadily enough and with it came the expected desperate contact with "on call" Governor to authorise staff call ins and breaking of our security protocols. Luckily as stated earlier when you have the experience of a Gunner or Blakey and the effervescence of a Mr. Bailey to call on you are well placed to get through any issues.

Whilst working behind the wall as part of a forgotten service has very unique issues. It most definitely is nothing like Porridge and we have never locked anyone up and thrown away the key. We in fact have a myriad of daily and in this case nightly care requirements that are one of the most fatiguing of all responses we face.

Unlike other areas of emergency and response the wait of a prison manager in night state is the wait of what is going to go wrong? When this is answered with any issue that requires a move external to the establishment, which is usually a hospital visit the speed of work required and impact on your staff and your own safety is huge.

More than the average of these events tend to crop up on my sets of nights but with each one I get a little better at dealing with them. As the week was drawing to a close the usual Christmas excess had been avoided for more than obvious reasons so the decision had been made to finish my last night with a run once relieved.

Sunday night quickly finished – my now customary purchased treats for the staff that had looked after me delivered and a more than acceptable relief had arrived well before 0700hrs Monday morning. Even the least bit of attention to these offerings would see that the venue could be only one place however the route was far from decided. Of the literally thousands of officers completing their nights there are scores of different ways of getting through that Monday. Differing from a couple of cans and sleep until they can't anymore, eating the postponed Sunday dinner and having a nap. I have even had notice of people stay up all the way through until they collapse at around 2100 on the Monday night with only coffee and sweets passing their lips.

As I pulled up at top car park, I was already in kit having changed at staff facilities and my route was set through the park and out to Ferriby and back. By no means one of my longest runs but a great kick start for the 2020 assault on my muffin top of a torso I had developed.

Bleary eyed, sugar filled and head a sharp as a tennis ball I set off. Even through the broken canopy of evergreen and bare trees I could see that this was going to be a morning of some beauty. As I came down Uncle Mike's steps, lapped the overwhelmed water areas up and over the tarmac incline to this time be met, fortuitously by an open gate leading on to the pathway to Ferriby. Thus, negating my previous dilemma of over or under whilst out with Cush and Stan.

Reaching the turnaround point at Ferriby of the flagpole I could feel an unseasonal warmth at my back as I readied to turn and find out the true wind direction. Two counts of luck hit as I felt nil wind meaning I was at the very least facing no resistance was coupled with one of the most perfect sunrises I had seen in a long time and certainly the most ever I had witnessed over the Estuary. Despite a quick pause to capture a snap on my phone of the sun between the towers of the span the run back into the Park was over in a relative flash. It was time now to slalom in between the early dog walkers and navigate back to the steps where this festive springboard into a training regime had begun. For this latest of ascents up this unforgiving stairway I had no partner, no encouragement from a throwaway insult, no call from a well minded passerby it was just me and my own effort. Moments like these are the reason I believe I will never stop training in some form. As I took off with whatever was left in my legs and hit the top in pretty good form. Considering the length and what the time had been since my last sleep I commended myself I only had left to end this latest visit to my church. Ending with a quick stride through the kissing gate across the seasonably sparsely populated car park, a stretch coupled with a change of top and taking of some fluids on board.

This completed I had the foundation set for another year of activity in, around and through Switzy.

19

The Flood

Even in the absence of our now cork dangling hat, wearing mate residing in the land of Paul Hogan and convicts. Our Sailor readying himself for the arrival of his beautiful daughter. Mr. Parker and I continued our Saturday morning ritual.

The content was often varied, a move away from the cards and more toward stamina as we were preparing for a duathlon but always had its roots in interval training of some sort. Stops at benches and steps still a staple test and of course opportunity to stretch our maturing frames.

This was the case for a long time until a period of wet weather hit the area and country so unprecedented that Hessles bizarre at best water table had no chance of handling. Already staring down the barrels of an extended at best football season due to pitches being completely inaccessible let alone playable.

The almost warren like number of different routes and levels that Switzy holds left me in the belief of having no issues in getting around with either Snowy or Mr. Parker for our respective exercise.

For long periods the regulars of Switzy have had an ability, a knowledge of the conditions therein and can predict the footwear required to complete their individual. Many a collective nod and amusement has been had between regulars at the sight of a young lad out to impress his new girl – skinny jeans, logo T-shirt completed with bright white trainers. Completely in the absence of a clue what the bowels of our playground had in store underfoot.

This run of weather broke with all logic weeks of seemingly endless downpours that were flooding Hessle

Recca and all open areas for as far as the eye could see. Our playground aside from a change from walking shoes to on occasion Wellies to combat a muddy and puddle strewn pathway Switzy appeared to be taking this in her stride.

I personally put a lot of this down to the recently felled trees and bushes in what was the second water area making a clear bowl for collection and was now filled back to my teenage days and severed back fame.

Then a three-day blast of rain changed this for what presents as for good, another walk completed, another circuit for me and Mr. Parker happened across these 3 days. With each engagement with our regulars there was a lot more "you won't get through there" and "it's under water" filling the conversations rather than the ritual "morning" or "good effort" shared on our respective laps.

Further into that spell I set off down the 99 steps to be confronted with a sight I had never seen in the time of the current layout of the park.

The two water areas that for years had not only been separate - and in the last 15 years plus the smaller area was arid dry – were now completely conjoined over spilled to the green areas. Water that had not only consumed the numerous benches, picnic areas and recently installed BBQ stands, but was raising up the steps.

Makeshift fishing pegs that were scattered around the larger water area now a thing of the past, signs that told of past and present occupants – of flora and fauna. Evidence of the working history of this bowl were only visible through the water level and not above it. Bins that stood tall enough to house domestic wheelie bins and then a foot above for aperture joined the other park furniture in being submerged.

The loop that serves dog walkers, park runners and fitness enthusiasts so well was now showing undulations as through its mile of odd shaped circumference stretched remained nothing but a little muddy. Whilst lower sections had become akin to secondary even third, fourth and fifth water areas of the park.

Even the start/finish point of the Park run was now a water feature to such a level that the tarmac slope was inaccessible and water filled to around 50 feet up, the incline. This presented a throwback of 35 plus years when I took my first tentative view of this area and looked into the water filled abyss in wonder at how I would ever get around it.

Knowledge of the layout and solid preparation in footwear allowed me to complete laps of the park and an in-tow cocker with a passion for swimming meant we lost little in the exercise during visits. However, it did curtail so much of others reason to come through the park.

Creativity is always seen at times like this and some of the more interesting sights seen have been a couple of lads in a canoe. Also, a fully wader clad master of a Labrador who had no interest in his human's desperate attempts in clinging on to the tree that was the only obstruction between himself and I reckon 30 feet of water.

Irony is at any time a split of humour and frustration but taking these accounts to modern day. Now at the point of us hitting dry green pitches around our area, a receding water level that now gives full access save for the water area to our park. Our country and across our globe we sit tight in the constraints of varying lockdown to help cease the spread of the viral threat of Covid-19.

Of the major restrictions being essential travel only, 1 period of activity per day, social distancing to a 2-meter radius and any gathering of more than 2 considered mass and excessive. What has been the very heart of people's reason to attend this is, temporarily at least, ruled against.

My walk on a sunny middle Saturday with my beautiful daughter and our ever willing Snowy gave confidence that at least in one area, my area people are abiding the rules that will see us back to "Normal". If that even is a thing in these times, sooner rather than later. The visitors to our park were clearly family, the cyclists passing through to conquer the bridge were lone, and the dog walker a bare minimum and most definitely not in the groups witnessed so regularly in the past.

The chat between my daughter and I was of a content I will never forget as my timeline memories that had just been viewed together. Memories that had shown pictures of messy eating, videos of the boy in charge of his vacuum and a capture of my princess finally recovering from the pneumonia that had her in its grip for a heartbreaking week. Simply we had covered everything.

My knowledge of a tree which the girls of year 6 are unlikely to ever be able to return for a last hair braiding session, haters and lovers on social media, Mummy's inability to complete a renegade dance are now on point. However, of all the chat that happened my daughter wanting to be outside, climbing, chatting and laughing not just with me but in my church gives a warmth nothing else can.

Switzy will return to its former glory complete with groups returning to have BBQs. Those wishing to complete their 3 laps in a Parkrun. Socially connect not isolate or distance with their respective 4-legged friends. A planned return by our Ferret will see his fellow Saturday morning club get the time off to make it a foursome once more and of course the original and best Bootcamp will ride again.

All of this will happen not because of lack of order or indeed instruction that stops them now, but simply because they want and will find a way.